Karen Killick.

NICE AND NASTY.

Steve Turner

First published 1980
by Razor Books and
Marshall Morgan & Scott Ltd.

Razor Books
10 Rectory Road
Crumpsall
Manchester 8

Marshall Morgan & Scott Ltd.
a Pentos company
1 Bath Street
London EC1V 9LB

ISBN 0 551 00865 2

Designed and illustrated by Philip Miles
Printed in Great Britain by
Hollen Street Press Ltd., Slough

CONTENTS

KEY WORDS AND PHRASES

impudent
perspective
decisions
natural processes

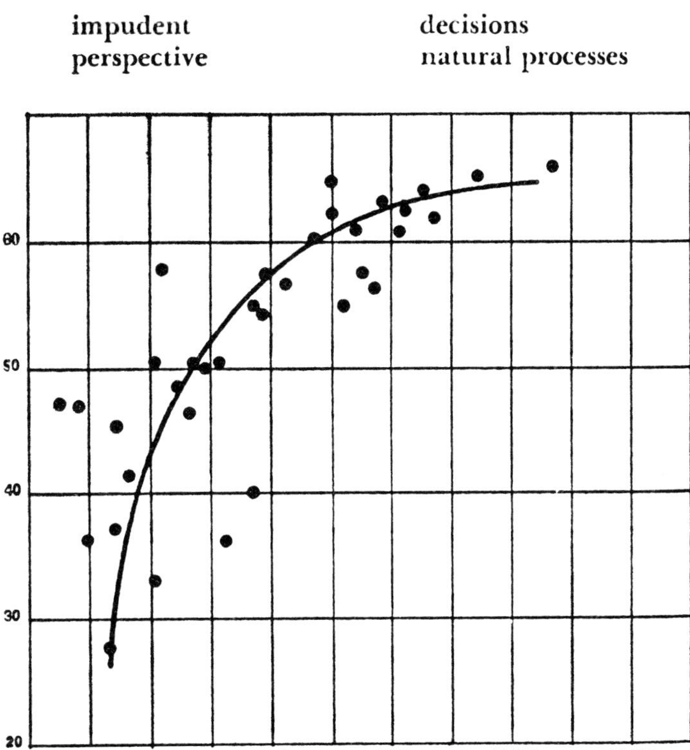

First Lessons in Living

These are your first lessons in living.
To begin we drag you head-first from your shelter,
away from your food, from your warmth.
We cut you apart from your only known friend.
We take you and beat you until strange gases
rush your lungs and pain jerks your frame.
These are your first lessons in living.
They will stand you in good stead.

Death Lib.

The liberating thing about death
is in its fairness to women,
its acceptance of blacks,
its special consideration
for the sick.

And I like the way
that children aren't excluded,
homosexuals are welcomed,
and militants aren't banned.

The really wonderful thing
about death
is that all major religions
agree on it, all beliefs
take you there, all philosophy
bows before it, all arguments
end there.

Con men can't con it
Thieves can't nick it
Bullies can't scare it
Magicians can't trick it.

Boxers can't punch it
Nor critics dismiss it
Don't knows can't not know
The lazy can't miss it.

Governments can't ban it
Or the army defuse it
Judges can't jail it
Lawyers can't sue it.

Capitalists can't bribe it
Socialists can't share it
Terrorists can't jump it
The Third World aren't spared it.

Scientists can't quell it
Nor can they disprove it
Doctors can't cure it
Surgeons can't move it.

Einstein can't halve it
Guevara can't free it
The thing about dead
Is we're all gonna be it.

A Way With Words

Had a way with words.
Seduced them from braincells
had them falling at his lips.
Had a way with women.
Spoke them like a language,
saw them understood.
And the words
worked on the women
and the women
turned into the words.
He had a way with
women and words
words and women,
although words never failed him.

Jilted

The first time
you are caught loving
in a just-friendly zone
they fine you
two eyes washed in tears
and a letter of appeal.
The next time it's three unpublished poems,
a few pounds in weight,
and an hour long discussion.
If it should happen
a third time
they have to withhold your feelings
so that you will learn
how to use them properly.

1974

Careful

Be careful
or the poet man
will come and
turn you into
the poem
he's just
writi

Something I've Never Said Before

I'm running short
of things I've never said
to anyone before.

It began with words
borrowed from filmscripts
and whispered in warm back rows.
Then I came up
with a few of my own
making them more serious
as the effects wore off.

It's many love poems later
and I'm low on originals.
There have been too many
only girls in the world,
too many confessions
meant at the time.

For you I had wanted
something new and unwrapped.
You deserved at least that.
Instead you must take this.
It is something
I have never said
to anyone before.

1973

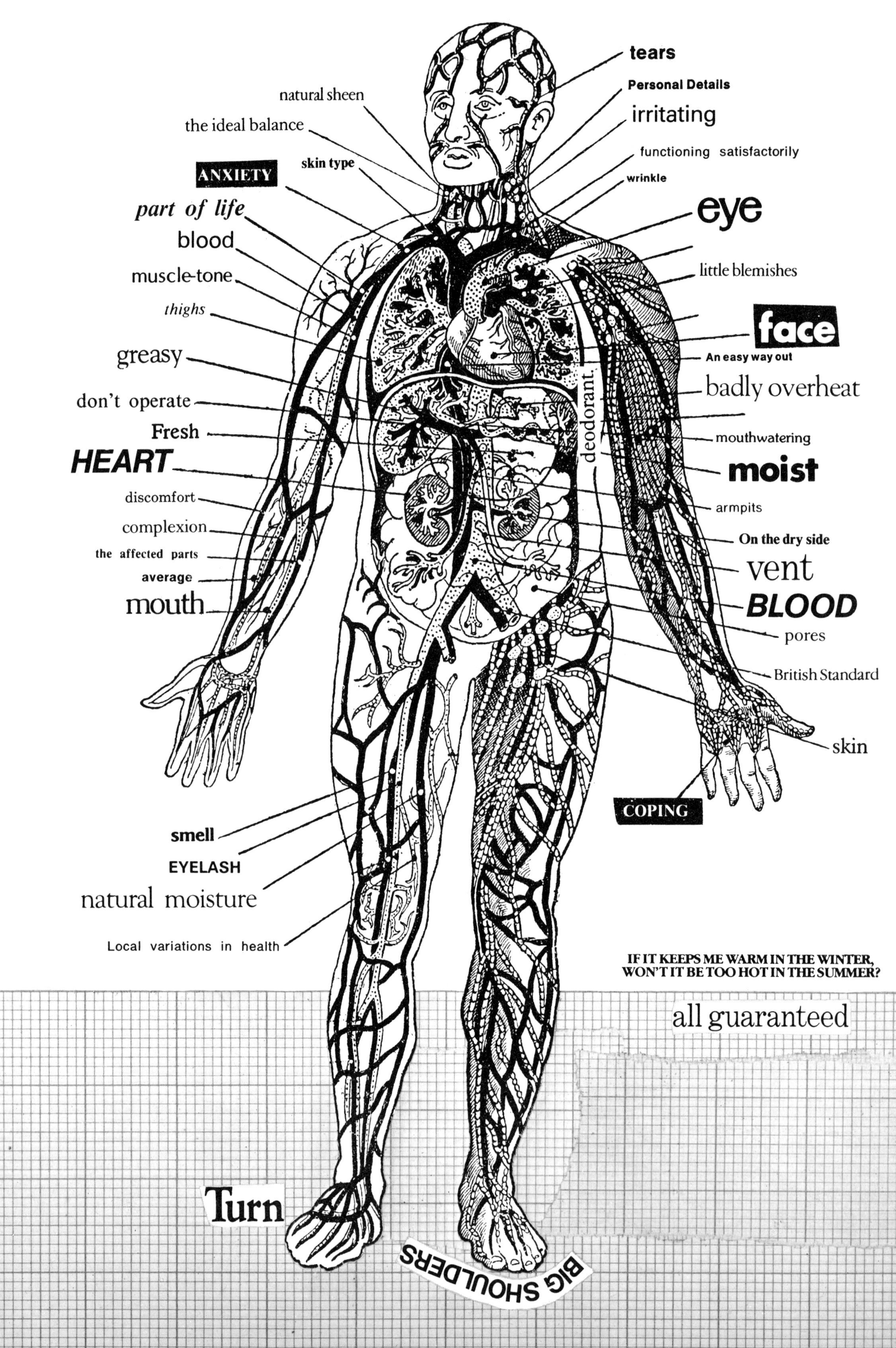
tears
Personal Details
natural sheen
irritating
the ideal balance
functioning satisfactorily
ANXIETY
skin type
wrinkle
part of life
eye
blood
little blemishes
muscle-tone
thighs
face
greasy
An easy way out
badly overheat
don't operate
deodorant.
Fresh
mouthwatering
HEART
moist
discomfort
armpits
complexion
On the dry side
the affected parts
vent
average
mouth
BLOOD
pores
British Standard
skin
COPING
smell
EYELASH
natural moisture
Local variations in health
IF IT KEEPS ME WARM IN THE WINTER,
WON'T IT BE TOO HOT IN THE SUMMER?
all guaranteed
Turn
BIG SHOULDERS

Blood Sweat And Tears

My blood knows where to go,
perspiration knows when to begin,
tears fall on cue.

If I were my blood
I'd take time off
every now and then,
take wrong turnings,
misinterpret instructions.

If I were perspiration
I'd arrive too soon,
hang around too long
and disappear when needed.

And if I were my tears
I'd forget to stock up,
I'd get low on salt
and leave without asking.

My body's in good shape.
It's upstanding and reliable.
We have so little in common.

New York City

Natural History

Most of us
do not go down
in history,
we just go down.
Our versions of
how things happened
perish behind our eyes.
Then our witnesses follow,
until the tip
of the last tongue
that we could be on
is swollen silent.
Years later,
children kicking leaves
in some church-yard
will subtract birthdays from deathdays
and laugh at old fashioned names
such as Stephen.

1975

A Few Thousand Days

One day the world
will carry on without me
just as it did
for the few thousand years
until Forty Nine.
I'd like to imagine
windows breaking of their own accord
on that day,
swollen eyed multitudes
pacing the streets,
a grey mist visiting the city,
everything somehow different,
incomplete.
But almost one hundred per cent
of the world
won't notice this new silence.
They will drink tea
and change trains
unaware that mankind
has been reshaped,
unaware that a few thousand days
just seeped through a hole
two seconds wide.

Tigers are the fiercest, the most ferocious. The number of peopl
NOW YOU MAY THINK THAT ANYONE
I love that old thing.
Well, I'll be back again same time tomorrow. Be ther
YOU'D BE RIGHT!
12:30

Hotel Radio on Low

Tigers are the fiercest, the most ferocious.
The number of people eaten by tigers each year.
To put that in perspective.
Are they really like big cats?
If you could stroke a tiger
it would be like stroking a cat.
Would it wag it's tail?
Moving their ears, and moving their whiskers!
Remember that cat lovers!
That was Michael Baw and he's a lecturer
at London Zoo.
How much illegal recording goes on?
This year a staggering 35,000.
This is staggering.
That, and of course the availability.
My grandfather specialised in comic songs
and monologues.
Now you may think that anyone
can play one of these, and you'd be right!
He had one in every one
of his jacket pockets.
Of course, his singing was much fruitier.
I love that old thing. I love it.
Well, I'll be back again at the same time tomorrow.
Be there, on the dot.

Cardiff

It Must Be Hard

It must be hard for those
whose faces make children cry,
whose voices make adults embarrassed,
whose skin turns our eyes to lovelier things.
They must get used to silence.
They must think of humans
as those who turn away,
who withdraw their smiles and sounds
like hands from an angry dog.
There is nothing as evil to us as ugliness.
It deserves only a room to hide itself in,
some air, and a little light.
Meanwhile, we help by telling
children not to stare
and by keeping our jokes to ourselves.

Washington D.C.

If Words Were Birds

If words
were birds
sentences
would fly
in formation
across page-white
skies.
Dictionaries would
have bars,
speeches
would darken
the sun.
If words
were birds
fly formation

sentences

skies across

page white dictionaries.

Bars

would have speeches.

Blacken the

would

sun.

I Am On The Kids' Side

I am on the kids' side
in the war against adults.
I don't want to stand still.
I don't want to sit still.
I don't want to be quiet.
I believe that strangers
are for staring at,
bags are for looking into,
paper is for scribbling on.
I want to know Why.
I want to know How.
I wonder What If.
I am on the kids' side
in the war against tedium.
I'm for going home
when stores get packed.
I'm for sleeping in
when parties get dull.
I'm for kicking stones
when conversation sags.
I'm for making noises.
I'm for playing jokes —
especially in life's
more Serious Bits.
I am on the kids' side.
See my sneaky grin,
watch me dance, see me run.
Spit on the carpet, rub it in,
pick my nose in public,
play rock stars in the mirror.
I am on the kids' side.
I want to know why we're not moving.
I'm fed up. I want to go out.
What's that? Can I have one?
It isn't fair. Who's that man?
It wasn't me, I was pushed.
When are we going to go?

I am on the kids' side
putting fun back into words.
Ink pink pen and ink
you go out because you stink.
Stephen Turner is a burner,
urner, murner, purner.
Stephen, weven, peven,
reven, teven, Turnip Top.
I am on the kids' side
in the war against apathy.
Mum, I want to do something.
It must be my turn next.
When can we go out?
I am on the kids' side
and when I grow up,
I want to be a boy.

People Who Love

You love her.
But she loves him.
He doesn't care.

So you write poems.
She writes songs.
He doesn't listen.

I love her
She loves no-one.
And no-one cares.

I write poems.
I write songs.
You listen.

The world is full
of poems and songs
and people
who love people
who love people
who don't love them.

History Lesson

History repeats itself.
Has to.
No-one listens.

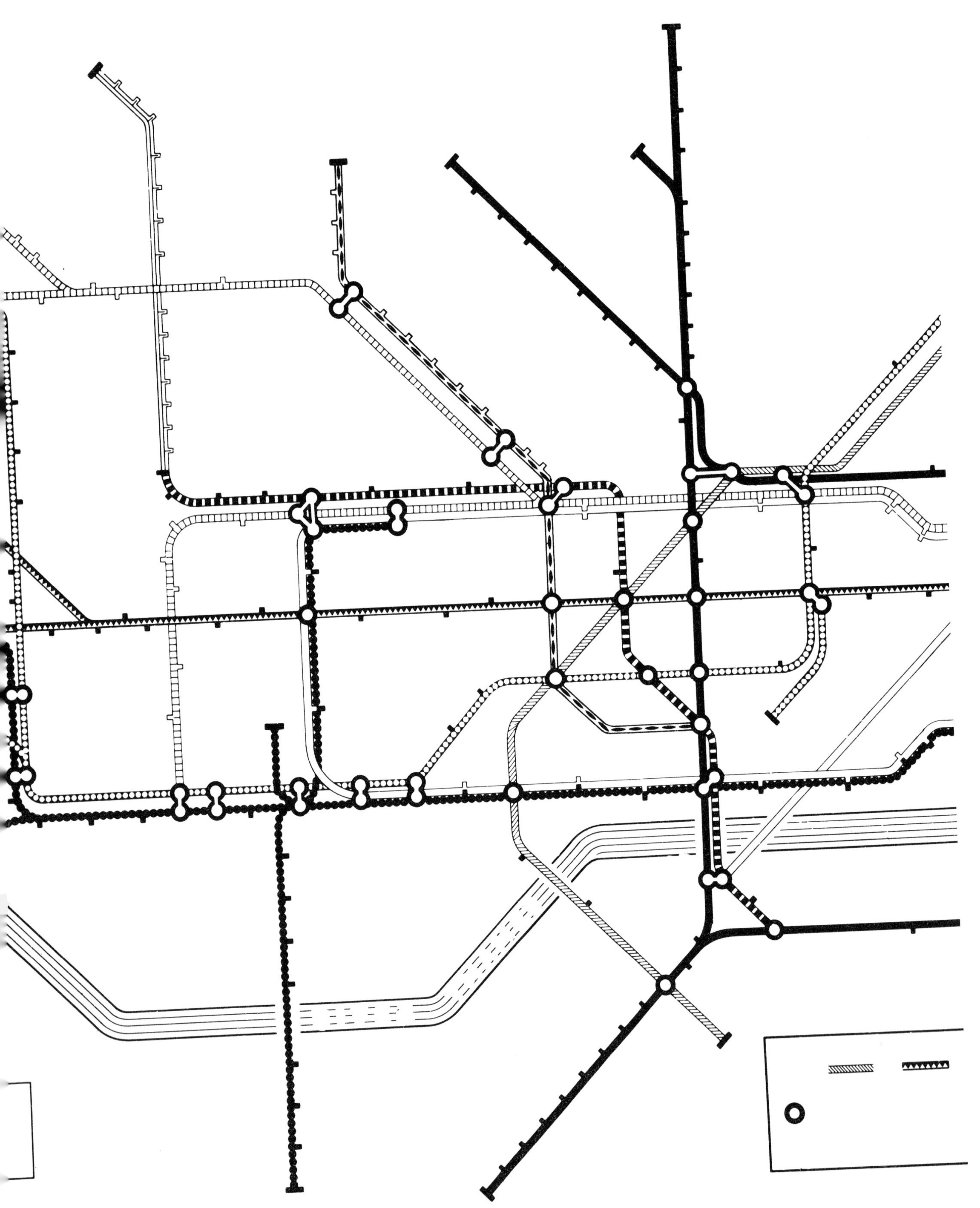

Shepherd Street W.1. RDP 282M OPEN
Antiques PARK Plumes Piccadilly W.1.
IN IN OUT OUT
Third Church of Christ The Scientist
Curzon Street Daska Sautters Pipes
Lebanon Libyan Arab Airlines
Keep Britain Tidy Keep Britain Tidy
Aphrodites Clarges Look Left
Look Left TMG 374M Bolton Street
DOG FOULS FOOTWAY FINE £20
Evening Standard On Sale Here
Midland Bank UNDERGROUND
TICKETS and TRAINS No Entry
This machine is temporarily out of order
This machine is temporarily out of order
This machine is temporarily out of order.
TICKETS IN IN IN Victoria Line
Yellow Tickets Take Ticket Here
The Comeback The Goodbye Girl
PLEASE STAND ON THE RIGHT
Eminently Male Oldham I'd be lost without it.
Pregnant. Terrific! Brilliant!
Where can you go for a walk? Spend more time
in the open. Well they said it couldn't happen.
PLEASE STAND ON THE RIGHT.
Lost London's greatest first class To stop
escalator PUSH I'd be lost without it
PLEASE STAND ON THE RIGHT
For those who prefer breast shaped bald facts
Madam Tussauds a nice person abortion help?
PLEASE STAND ON THE RIGHT
Two new London Transport Books Jack Jones
Portrait of A Man
PLEASE STAND ON THE RIGHT
Victoria Line Northbound
No Smoking No Smoking No Smoking
Private. Keep the doorway clear.
Green Park
Green Park Green Park
Green Park Green Park Green Park
Green Park Green Park Green Park Green Park.

Council for the Protection of Rural England, 4 Hobart Place,
Preservation Society,
Commons, Open Spaces and Footpaths

Backs To Nature

You could tell it was spring
when the first egg of Easter
burst on to the counter.
You could tell it was summer
by the gradual lengthening
of ice cream queues.
Supermarket folklore had it
that autumn was heralded
by the migration of sunglasses
into the store room
and that you could tell
it was winter by the first fall
of tinsel.
You could tell we were alive
by the condensation on the mirrors,
the way our reflections moved
on the window's darkened face.

Love And Nothing

Love
can let
you down
but
nothing
never gets
worse.

New York

Decreation (The Big Bang Theory)

On the eighth day our rest was disturbed
by the drumming of machinery;
pistons pumping, wheels spinning,
smoke spuming in the sky.
On the ninth day they made us into
the image of animals, offspring of stray gasses,
cosmic bastards in the gigantic unplanned family of Man.
On the tenth day sick waters wretched
and vomited their fish onto the sands.
Rivers expired, whales split
and the fate of seals was sealed.
On the eleventh day the moon lost her virginity.
Her mystery is gone.
Inside her womb you will find a flag, equipment
and the footprints of Adam.
On the twelfth day the earth was burgled
and its riches went missing.
The Western World was observed
leaving the scene of the crime.
On the thirteenth day you could not see for miles
because the bad breath of civilisation
hung like gauze curtains in the sky.
On the morning of the fourteenth day
we rehearsed for the end of the world
on the open deserts and beneath the mountains.
By lunchtime our armies were massed on the borders
waiting to go out and play,
waiting to add that finishing touch.

The Lying Blues

Woke up in the morning
With lies on my radio
Woke up in the morning
With lies on my radio
Said — Don't be uptight 'cos everything is alright
If you just stay tuned to my show

Got up and caught the train
But lies stood along the line
Got up and caught the train
But lies stood along the line
They said if I soak up lungs full of smoke
Health and happiness will be mine

Saw the morning paper
Where the lies weren't hard to find
Saw the morning paper
Where the lies weren't hard to find
It said that show biz, TV, sport and nudies,
Were all that happened all the time

Down at the disco
Were the same lies with a beat
Down at the disco
Were the same lies with a beat
Sayin' feelin' good is bein' good
So live your life like you move your feet

Looked at my TV
They had experts telling lies
Looked at my TV
They had experts telling lies
But you couldn't tell, it was done so well,
Being expert is a great disguise

Looked at the adverts
They were lies all dressed to kill
Looked at the adverts
They were lies all dressed to kill
I dropped my guard to give a laugh out loud
And they came in and took my will

Bought me a magazine
And it's lies were done with class
Bought me a magazine
And it's lies were done with class
They said it's ok most people do today
If it feels good just don't ask.

Just One More Time

Lead me into temptation
just one more time.
Lead me up close
through circumstances
beyond my control.
Lead me then leave me.
Deliver me from escape,
increase my ignorance,
limit my will.
Make me the victim of
a victim-less crime.
Leave me 'til sin
is the only way out,
give me a taste of
what to avoid.
Leave me 'til it's
your fault
yet guilt floods me
like a chill.
Then lead me back
into temptation,
just one more time.

How To Hide Jesus

There are people after Jesus.
They have seen the signs.
Quick, let's hide Him.
Let's think; carpenter,
                fishermen's friend,
                disturber of religious comfort.
Let's award Him a degree in theology,
a purple cassock
and a position of respect.
They'll never think of looking here.
Let's think;
His dialect may betray Him,
His tongue is of the masses.
Let's teach Him Latin
and seventeenth century English,
they'll never think of listening in.
Let's think;
humble,
Man Of Sorrows,
nowhere to lay His head.
We'll build a house for Him,
somewhere away from the poor.
We'll fill it with brass and silence.
It's sure to throw them off.

There are people after Jesus.
Quick, let's hide Him.

Jerusalem

The Ritz Piccadilly, W1 (01-493 8181). Re-gilded Palm Court is a must for tea and the dining room is equally majestic. (£20·00)

Death Sex Religion And Politics

I'm afraid we don't talk about death here,
not while drinking tea.
Death is a private matter.
It's up to the individual.
Thinking about it won't make it any easier.
You can worry yourself to death
but not back again.
Sex is a private matter too.
People shouldn't have problems.
I learned everything I needed through jokes at school.
Thinking about it doesn't make it any easier.
Sex is another thing we don't talk about.
Religion? Well, each man to his own, I say.
It's bad manners to argue religion.
They all lead to God.
There's no difference between Buddhism and frog worship.
I learned all I need to know about religion at school.
You can worry yourself to death but not to heaven.
I'm afraid we don't discuss politics here.
Politics is a private matter
like sex and death.
Like all religions, all politicians are the same.
They all lead to death.
I learned all I need to know about bad manners
at school.

The Fact

In the end not much is needed.
In the end not much is possible.
The globe has shrunk
to the size of a room.
A room is shrinking
to the size of a bed.
The walls have moved closer,
the roof is descending,
a lamp stands on the horizon.
In the end
there is sleeping and waking.
There is eating, reading, thinking.
It was like this in the beginning too,
except there was no reading
and little to think on.
In the end is the beginning
and in the beginning was the end.
In the between are houses, holidays,
wars, wives, diversions.
In the end
it is like it has always been
yet activity obscured the fact.

How Fitting (Joseph Martin 1883-1978)

How fitting
to become a child
before this leap
into eternity.
How fitting
that at this end
it is so much like
the beginning.
Again they bring
you food and wipe
away the traces.
Again a walk
from chair to door
seems like a journey,
buttons are hard work,
dressing is an art.
How fitting
that this largest part
of eternity
should take you
as a child.

Old Soldier (Joseph Martin 1883-1978)

I am bent and creased
although I never liked
things bent or creased.
The years they have
untidied me,
they have left me strewn.
My skin has
become one size too large
like a shirt I would return.
My bones have shrunk
inside me
as if washed once too often.
The years, they have it in
for old soldiers.
They snipe at our pride.
Can't go on parade like this.
Have to sit it out
in the barrack room.
Have to sit it out in the chair.

Sitting There Trying Not To Write You A Poem

I'd only known you
for one party,
two films,
three drinks and
a telephone conversation
but there I was
straining for a poem.
That's the real
hard stuff, poetry.
It takes so much
to come off
once you get on.

1974

High Altitude Infatuation

You were
five and a half feet
above London.
I was 33,000
feet above Athens
or somewhere like that.
Five hundred
miles an hour,
ground speed.
Twenty minutes
behind time.
I was writing.
I was head down,
writing posture.
Your perfume
walked past me
in the aisle.
I looked up
and there was
your perfume
walking past me.

cut out their heads and paste them onto other pictures of sexy female bodies. I get aroused doing this

– they were naked, packed together,

—a masterpiece of sex, terror, murder and more sex

), and, for S/M enthusiasts,

, "I rarely saw them as individuals.

as soon as they were naked –

the live whips-and-chains show

).

continues to flourish as the place to get it on without guilt.

they were no longer human beings

she doesn't mind being a 'sex object'? 'Hardly!

ab-stractions to me,

I love it!

not human beings

uncensored pictures including shots of

. Things that would have shocked and horrified me in 1934,

. Am I sick, or is my behavior within the limits of normal sexuality?—

. Keep it to yourself and you'll do OK. If not, you'd better see a shrink.

No Longer Human Beings

Cut off their heads
and paste them onto
other pictures
of sexy female bodies.
I get aroused doing this.
They were naked, packed together,
a masterpiece of sex, terror,
murder and more sex.
And for S/M enthusiasts
I rarely saw them as individuals
As soon as they were naked live
whips and chains show
It continues to flourish as
the place to get it on without guilt
They were no longer human beings
She doesn't mind being a sex object
Hardly! They were abstractions to me.
I love it! Not human beings
Uncensored pictures including shots of
Things that would have horrified me in 1934
Am I sick or is my behaviour
within the limits of normal sexuality?
Keep it to yourself and you'll do OK.
If not you'd better see a shrink.

*(Cut-up from interviews with Nazis
Albert Speer and Franz Stangl plus random
copy from Playboy and Penthouse)*

Where Jesus Touched The Earth

I went to see where Jesus
once touched the earth
but the Catholics
had got there before me
and obscured His footprints
with arches, buttresses,
gold and incense.

I went to see where Jesus
once touched the earth.
I couldn't see for
concrete and collection boxes,
for postcards and guide books.

So I looked further down.
I looked to the ground.
But the ground was thirty feet
higher than back in A.D. 3.
This is not where Jesus walked.

I looked down, down to my feet,
my legs, arms, chest.
I looked down to where Jesus
touches the earth.

Jerusalem

History Lesson

History repeats itself.
Has to.
No-one listens.

London : Wednesday
March 12
Price : Ten pence

Evening
STANDARD

CLOSING PRICES

Time to go . . . are you ready?

POET TELLS OF HIS DEATH

My Tragic Untimely Death

Whichever way I go, whatever year I leave,
it will be untimely.
Whether by heart or lung, knife or axe,
or simply Life's refusal to loan me new cells
— all of it, just at the wrong moment
— all of it, a tragic way to die.
There will be something left undone,
some people I wanted to see, and besides,
the room won't be in a fit condition
for relations to look around.
At that poem, half finished in pencil under the bed,
— they won't publish that will they?
Is it ridden with ominous signs,
thinly disguised farewells?
And even this poem. Am I tempting fate?
A fitting end no doubt for this to be found
beside my body.
It could get me in the papers, in italics of course,
POET TELLS OF HIS DEATH in bold type
plus a photograph taken at twenty two.
But when it does come
it will be when I've stopped counting.
It will be the very day I feel least death-like,
not the one when I shake hands
to leave lasting impressions,
and tidy away my belongings just in case.

One

Black and legless.
Disco radio
in the wheelchair.
His head dances
to the beat.

Two

Shabby as a sidewalk.
Asking for a quarter.
You are a failure.
You are un-American.

Three

Sometimes his mother
must have held him high.
Only the best was good enough.
It's important to remember this.

Four

This year's thing.
Last year's thing.
Next year's thing.
This year's thing.
Next year's thing.
Last year's thing.

Five

Someone needs
an ambulance.
Whyee
Whyee
Whyee
Whyee
Whyee?

Six

Hey,
I like the way
you talk.
You from Ingerland?
Yeahh?

Seven

Feel a thought
coming on.
Must take
some television.

Chance

If chance be
the Father of all flesh,
disaster is his rainbow in the sky,
and when you hear

state of emergency
sniper kills ten
troops on rampage
whites go looting
bomb blasts school

it is but the sound of man
worshipping his maker.

New York

'Religion Is The Opium Of The People'

This opium is dangerous.
Colourless, odourless,
and smuggled in the heart
nevertheless this opium
is dangerous.
It changes people,
it will turn our children into enemies.
This opium makes them mad.
They start seeing things,
imagining the world big with spirit,
long with heaven.
They start to fantasise,
imagine there's more than meets the eye.
This opium makes them joyous.
You can tell if they have this opium.
Listen for their singing,
look closely in their eyes,
hear them whisper in the air.
They lose all interest
in making money
or conquering the world.
They lose all interest in us
when they discover this opium.
We have them registered now.
They are eighty per cent of us.
We shall watch them closely.
The public must not be infected.

Houses Without Faces

Houses without faces
Houses without faces
Boarded up eyes
Corrugated teeth
Houses without faces
Houses without faces
You can do so much
When you haven't got a face
You can hide so much
when you haven't got a face
Houses without faces
Houses without faces
Boarded up eyes
Corrugated teeth
People without faces
Faces without people
Boarded up people
Corrugated people
Burned out people
Masked up people
People without faces
Houses without people
Houses with people
People without houses
People without houses
Burned out of their houses
Burned out terraced houses
Houses without faces
Houses without faces

Belfast

The Poem To End All Wars

This is the poem
to end all wars,
the one that proves
bullets a likely
cause of death
and death a cause
of sorrow.
The one that points out
connections between
anger and bent fingers,
bent fingers and triggers,
triggers and sorrow,
bent fingers and tears,
anger and sorrow.
The one that says;
to avoid tears
do not bend fingers
but raise hands in air,
wave, clap, embrace,
shake hands, smile, clap,
wave, raise hands in air.
The one that makes it easy.
The one that forgets fingers
obey the shape of the heart.
The one we have all written
at some time or other.

In The Interests Of National Security

It is wrong
to be wrong
unless
you are wrong
while protecting
the right people
from wrong.
Then it is
alright to be wrong
because rulers
have the rights
on what is right
and there's no-one
big enough
to tell a ruler
what is wrong.
Right?

(Wrong)

1975 Los Angeles

If Jesus Was Born Today

If Jesus was born today
it would be in a downtown motel
marked by a helicopter's flashing bulb.
A traffic warden, working late,
would be the first upon the scene.
Later, at the expense of a TV network,
an eminent sociologist,
the host of a chat show
and a controversial author
would arrive with their good wishes
— the whole occasion to be filmed as part of the
'Is This The Son Of God?' one hour special.
Childhood would be a blur of photographs
and speculation
dwindling by His late teens into
'Where Is He Now?' features in Sunday magazines.

If Jesus was thirty today
they wouldn't really care about the public ministry,
they'd be too busy investigating His finances
and trying to prove He had Church or Mafia
connections.
The miracles would be explained by
an eminent and controversial magician,
His claims to be God's Son recognised as
excellent examples of Spoken English
and immediately incorporated into the O-Level syllabus,
His sinless perfection considered by moral philosophers
as, OK, but a bit repressive.

If Jesus was thirty-one today
He'd be the fly in everyone's ointment —
the sort of controversial person who
stands no chance of eminence.
Communists would expel Him, capitalists
would exploit Him or have Him
smeared by people who know a thing or two about God.
Doctors would accuse Him of quackery,
soldiers would accuse Him of cowardice,
theologians would take Him aside and try
to persuade Him of His non-existence.

If Jesus was thirty-two today we'd have to
end it all. Heretic, fundamentalist, literalist,
puritan, pacifist, non-conformist, we'd take Him
away and quietly end the argument.
But the argument would rumble in the ground
at the end of three days and would break out
and walk around as though death was some bug,
saying 'I am the resurrection and the life.
No man cometh to the Father but by me'.
While the magicians researched new explanations
and the semanticists wondered exactly what
He meant by 'I' and 'No-one' there would be those
who stand around amused, asking for something
called proof.

62 **Exclusive Pictures**

Give us good pictures
of the human torch
which show the skin
burnt like chicken,
bursting like grapes.

It will teach us
to avoid flames.

Give us good film
of the lady on the ledge
as she leaps open mouthed
and hits the streets
like a suicide.

It will teach us
to use stairways.

Give us sharp colour
coverage of the African
troubles. Show us
interesting wounds,
craters in fat and flesh.

It will teach us
not to point guns.

Give us five page spreads
of the airliner that fell
like a pigeon to the ground.
And make sure you get there
before the victims are pulled out.

It will teach
engines to function.

Don't give us
any of that shaky
hand-held stuff
where the trapped children
are smoke-like shapes
and their screams barely audible
beneath the wailing sirens.
Get in there with your lenses
and your appetite for danger
and your hard news head
and give us what we're after.
Make us informed.
Make us feel we're really there.
Provide us with education.
Broaden our backgrounds.
We live in a democracy
and we need to know.

Left Right

Left right Left right
Left right Left right

I was getting worried
Couldn't sleep at night
'Cos I didn't quite know
If I was left or right
So feel my leanings
Test my views
Check my reactions
to the Ten o'Clock News

Should I buy the Mirror
Or should I buy The Sun
The Times Literary
Or The Guardian?
Will I be a fascist
If I use the police
Or will I be a commie
If I march for peace?
Who is it I follow
If I'm down on porn
Begin a Foetus Lib
For the not yet born?

Feel my leanings
Test my views
Check my reactions
to the Ten o'Clock News
Am I middle class
Or am I alright
Get me tested
Am I left or right?
Get me tested
Am I left or right?

Send me all the questions
Mail me all the forms
Fix me up a blood test
Tell me all the rules
I've got to know now
Put my mind at rest

Am I of the right
Or am I communist?
Please make me something
I've been nothing too long
I need to find out
If I'm left or wrong.

Watch my language
Hear my views
Check my reactions
To the Six o'Clock News
Am I working class
And am I alright
Get me tested
Am I left or right?
Get me tested
Am I left or right?

They Had It Coming

The South East Asians,
they were made to cry,
Look at their eyes all
narrowed up and ready to bawl.
Black Africans.
Obesity wouldn't suit them.
There's a grace about their
slenderness.
Their children would be naked
without a covering of flies.
Indians are perfect for begging
in ragged clothes
and falling dead on the streets
without too much sensation.
There are so many of them
that death is no longer a problem.
Middle Easterners, South Americans,
they were made to look anguished,
the mother crying to God,
the children just crying.
Earthquakes provide opportunity
for this.
White Westerners were made to laugh
in fast cars with beautiful friends.
They were made to drink and spend money.
Do not disturb the balance of nature.

Wait

These are
the good
old days.

Just wait
and see.

Short Poem

Short poems
are fun.
You can see
at a glance
whether you
like them
or not.

false. A new eye-opening offer What goes on under

the changing styles of the twentieth century

...overnment ... sat ... e First Bap-
...hurch of Washingto... ...hile his host,
...resident of the Un... States, con-
...d a Sunday School ... on *I Kings*
Even to secular ey... ...his turn of
...s might seem mi... ...ous; to the
...Georgi Vins, 50, it ... ...ite literally
... of God.

...ins is an uncompro... ...ng Baptist
...rade that brought hi... ...d four oth-
...viet prisoners of co... ...ence to the
...in return for two sp... ...ent back to
...viet Union, has pre... ...d the world
...a new sort of religio... ...itness. The
...y preacher and poet ... ...o spent sev-
... the past 15 years i... ...eria, is the
...leader of the tens ... ...ousands of
...away "Reform Ba... ..." to reach
...West. Fourteen year... ..., they for-
... seceded from the g... ...nment-rec-
...ed All-Union Counc... ...Evangelical
...tians-Baptists in or... ...to fight for
... religious freedom th... ...Moscow per-
... In an interview wi... ...IME's John
...n, Vins painted a... ...traordinary
...ait of a beleaguered ... ...ious move-
... and of a life that in ... ...e ways re-
... letters of the impr... ...ed Apostle
...o the early church.

...Our situation is diffic... ...or Western
...ians to understand, ... says. Since
...ys of John Bunyan ... Roger Wil-
... Baptists have tradit... ...lly believed
...al separation of ch... and state.
...ttempts to practice ... belief have
...ard treatment in the ... ...viet Union.
...sts who follow Sovie... ...es can hold
...ip services, but the g... ...nment for-
...them to preach the ... of God in
...c or to bring up thei... ...ldren with
...ous instruction.

...lthough they have be... ...riven by re-
...s conscience into resi... Moscow's
...res, the Reform Ba... insist that
...re not political diss... ...ts. "In ac-
...nce with biblical t... ...ing," Vins

searc... ...iev until he dedicat... ...self
full ti... religious work in 196...
W... Vins calls a strong ... ...ptist
awak... ..." was occurring ... ...ally
amon... young, partly in resp... to a
virule... ...tichurch campaign t... ...eing
condu... by Soviet Party Ch... ...kita
Khru... ...v. Obviously unde... ...ong

Soviet ... ...st Leader Georgi Vins
In the ... ...tion of Roger William...

pressu... ...e All-Union Counc... ...ered
Baptis... keep children from ... ...ing

control that puts you in control When you can't say goodbye

ment's le...
directs th...
But in 19...
Novosibi...
cy in ret...
KGB, Vin...
harsh lab...
After tha...
five more...
liberation...
In de...
cret activ...
mobile ...
Khristian...
the coun...
bles and ...
ually bu...
ton or ...
place. Th...
ing team...
set press...
ried in s...
permit ...
estants. ...
correspo...
ganizatio...
religious...
work in...
ings, hel...
tract a th...

Vins' ...
agai...
if anyth...
viet Un...
side. Th...
other in...
thought ...
terprodu...
Council. ...
es. "If e...
might v...
recent p...
his own ...
edly aft...
ing for h...

For Georgi Vins, The Day After His Release

Already I'm beginning to wonder
when freedom will lose it's bright glow for you.
Today you must be delirious with smiling faces,
open Bible, open street, open door, open gospel,
open church.
But already I'm beginning to wonder
when you'll notice that the palms are thinning out
on the dusty road from Siberia.
I'm beginning to wonder
when you'll see that there are never any fingerprints
in the hotel Gideon.
I'm beginning to wonder
when you'll walk the streets of New York
and whether you'll go out alone.
I'm beginning to wonder
whether you'll hear secret police
whistling tunes in elevators and supermarkets
in a carefully conceived plan
to stop the private ownership of thoughts.
I'm beginning to wonder
when you'll see your first millionaire evangelist
asking for more money to stay on TV
so that he can ask for more money to stay on TV.
I'm beginning to wonder
when you'll pass your first State church
closed by the people.
I'm beginning to wonder
when they'll let you meet the victims of freedom,
persecuted by apathy, exiled within themselves.

Los Angeles

Stuck At Seventeen (Rock'n Roll Poem)

Hey mum I'm all grown up
Yet I feel like a kid
Must be something I ate
Or something that you did
I'm going on thirty
And I'm stuck at seventeen
Should be into grey suits
And I'm still wearing jeans

You said that rock'n roll
Was an adolescent phase
That sprung up like a spot
And disappeared in days
You said I'd see sense
Then turn into a man
Try Tchaikovsky
Throw my records in the can

But I'm all grown up and I'm stuck at seventeen
You'll never make me different from the way I've always been
I'm all grown up and I'm stuck at seventeen
I'm an innocent delinquent and rock'n rolling being

You showed me winklepickers
and the cramping of the toes
Losses of employment
Through the colour of me clothes
Possible delinquency
By wearing tapered jeans
Effects of rock'n roll
Upon impressionable teens

You really did your best
To try and make me get well
With those sensible shoes
And the tubes of Trugel
With the nice sons of friends
and some hymns with a beat
And modern brown sandals
To give me healthy feet.

But I'm all grown up and I'm stuck at seventeen
You'll never make me different from the way I've always been
I'm all grown up and I'm stuck at seventeen
I'm an innocent delinquent and a rock'n rolling being

But nothin' really worked
I'm in a leather jacket
I tried wearin' ties but
my neck couldn't hack it
Don't wait for Steve mother
He's never gonna grow
He's gonna be like Johnny
And just Go, Go, Go.

Not

Thick around
the middle,
not fat.
Receding,
not going bald.
Tired eyes,
not failing sight.
Maturing features,
not wrinkled skin.
Growing older,
not dying.

Waterlow, Massachusetts.

Christmas Is Really For The Children

Christmas is really
for the children.
Especially for children
who like animals, stables,
stars and babies wrapped
in swaddling clothes.
Then there are wise men,
kings in fine robes,
humble shepherds and a
hint of rich perfume.

Easter is not really
for the children
unless accompanied by a
cream filled egg.
It has whips, blood, nails,
a spear and allegations
of body snatching.
It involves politics, God
and the sins of the world.
It is not good for people
of a nervous disposition.
They would do better to
think on rabbits, chickens
and the first snowdrop
of spring.
Or they'd do better to
wait for a re-run of
Christmas without asking
too many questions about
what Jesus did when he grew up
or whether there's any connection.

1.0 FARMING.
1.25 MR SMITH PROPAGATES PLANTS.
1.50 NEWS.
1.55 FILM: IT'S A MAD, MAD, MAD, MAD, WORLD. See film guide).
4.25 BUGS BUNNY.
4.40 THE HIGH CHAPARRAL.
5.30 EMU'S BROADCASTING COMPANY.
5.55 NEWS.
6.05 THE CHILDREN OF THE NEW FOREST.
6.35 APPEAL.
6.40 YOUR SONGS OF PRAISE CHOICE.

10.40
10.50
11.30
12.10-
SCOTL
except
on be
Park
Childre
WALES
1.55-2
With B
4.25 S

BBC 2

7.40-1.55 OPEN UNIVERSITY.
1.55 CRICKET. Essex v Yorkshire.
6.45 NEWS REVIEW.
7.15 THE COMMAND-

Marilyn slips her arm through his, giggles happily and says: "Darling, you're not talking about the poor again."

The Appeal

Don't give them your money.
They don't really need it.
It'll only create problems.
We need helpless people
and money wipes them out.
Too much food
and they'll have to
bring in the slimming pills.
Too much success
and they'll have to
fly in psychiatrists.
These folk have found the simple life,
the open-air life, the life
unencumbered by possessions,
by status.
Don't export the
curse of affluence
to the Third World.
They'll only become like us
or, if we give too freely,
we'll become like them.

Birth

I didn't ask
to be born.
I wasn't even
there to ask.
When you are born
you can ask for
anything.
Almost anything.
You cannot ask
to be unborn.
If you do
there is very little
that can be done.
I didn't ask
to be born.
I was under age
at the time.
My parents had
to decide
on my behalf.
I'm glad that
I was born.
You have to be born
to be glad.

1973

History Lesson

History repeats itself.
Has to.
No-one listens.

I want to be free from
any emotional ties

Dear Steve, I have
been thinking things
over since we last
meet and have come
to the decision that I
don't won't to go out
with you any more.

Letter Bomb

Take care.
It is not
always possible
to detect them
at first glance.
They weigh as much
as circulars
or income tax demands.
Take care.
Normally they start
with a Dear where
a Dearest used to be.
They go on to say
something about not
knowing how to put it.
They put it.
They hope you're not hurt.
You are.
Take care.
Do not plunge the package
into a brine-soaked
handkerchief.
Withdraw.
Call for assistance.

"It's all for the best."
"Time is a great healer."

1973

After You'd Gone

No-one
like you.
That then
the pleasure.
That now
the pain.

Washington D.C.

Truth

There's no
such thing
as truth.

No.
Not even
this.

1974

DEAD

People Who Die

People who die in disasters,
like people who get themselves murdered,
are not really people.
Their photographs prove it;
always slightly out of focus
taken in gardens we do not know,
resorts we would not visit.
They come from towns
we have never been to.
They leave relations
with funny names.
They led 'quiet lives'
and had 'few close friends'.
People who are reported missing
like people who fall dead in the street
are not really people.
Like extra-terrestrial life
they never come from your street.
Like extra-terrestrial life
they are news, but only for a day.

1975

Jingles

Absence makes the
heart grow fonder.

Get ABSENCE.

Out of sight is
out of mind.
Girl, you are
outtasight.

Everything

Looks aren't everything.
Luxury's not everything.
Money's not everything.
Health is not everything.
Success is not everything.
Happiness is not everything.
Even everything is not everything.
There's more to life than everything.

1975

The Photographs

They take them away.
That's what's so frightening.
One moment they're happy,
as the photographs show,
and then they are taken
behind the tall walls,
along cold passageways,
to the places we do not go.
What happens next is
a medical secret
but has to do with ageing
in a very short time.
What happens next is
the mortician's secret.
One moment they're happy,
as the photographs show,
and then they are
words carved in stone
on freshly broken ground.
Look at the photographs.
Look at their eyes.
Look at their smiles.
IT'S BEHIND YOU! we shout,
it's behind you.

Earl Grosvenor — heir to a reputed £500 millions fortune — and his wife, Natalia, leaving Heathrow yesterday for Canada en route for a honeymoon in Hawaii. They were married on Saturday

Five Hundred Million Pounds

The Earl of Grosvenor
has five hundred million pounds.
He is honeymooning in Hawaii.
He has five hundred million pounds
and he still has to honeymoon
in the world.
He has married Natalia.
She is not my sort of girl.
Five hundred million pounds
and he marries someone
who is not my sort of girl.
The Earl of Grosvenor
carries a black case
in his right hand.
Five hundred million pounds
and he still has to carry
a black case in his right hand.
It is probably heavy.
He will probably sweat.
Damp patches will form
beneath his arms
as if he were a construction worker
or an unemployed gentleman
carrying a black case.
I expect his shoes hurt sometimes.
I expect he forgets his handkerchief.
I expect he wonders whether Natalia
really love him.
I expect he wonders what it would be like
to have only four hundred and fifty
million pounds.
The Earl of Grosvenor takes off.
He wonders whether the engines will catch fire.
He knows you can't pay engines off.
He knows that the ocean is indifferent to millionaires.
Five hours in the air and he is restless.
Five hundred million pounds and he is restless.

Creed

We believe in Marxfreudanddarwin.
We believe everything is OK
as long as you don't hurt anyone,
to the best of your definition of hurt,
and to the best of your knowledge.

We believe in sex before during
and after marriage.
We believe in the therapy of sin.
We believe that adultery is fun.
We believe that sodomy's OK.
We believe that taboos are taboo.

We believe that everything's getting better
despite evidence to the contrary.
The evidence must be investigated.
You can prove anything with evidence.

We believe there's something in horoscopes,
ufo's and bent spoons;
Jesus was a good man just like Buddha
Mohammed and ourselves.
He was a good moral teacher although we think
his good morals were bad.

We believe that all religions are basically the same,
at least the one that we read was.
They all believe in love and goodness.
They only differ on matters of
creation sin heaven hell God and salvation.

We believe that after death comes The Nothing
because when you ask the dead what happens
they say Nothing.
If death is not the end, if the dead have lied,
then it's compulsory heaven for all
excepting perhaps Hitler, Stalin and Genghis Khan.

We believe in Masters and Johnson.
What's selected is average.
What's average is normal.
What's normal is good.

We believe in total disarmament.
We believe there are direct links between
warfare and bloodshed.
Americans should beat their guns into tractors
and the Russians would be sure to follow.

We believe that man is essentially good.
It's only his behaviour that lets him down.
This is the fault of society.
Society is the fault of conditions.
Conditions are the fault of society.

We believe that each man must find the truth
that is right for him.
Reality will adapt accordingly.
The universe will readjust. History will alter.
We believe that there is no absolute truth
excepting the truth that there is no absolute truth.

We believe in the rejection of creeds,
and the flowering of individual thought.

Books by Steve Turner

Tonight We Will Fake Love (poetry) Charisma Books 1974 / Razor Books 1978
Conversations with Eric Clapton Abacus 1976
A Decade of The Who (text only) Elmtree/Essex Music 1977

What they said about *Tonight We Will Fake Love*

"At last, a poet who captures today with all the flair of a rock number."

Peter Lewis *Daily Mail*

"There are lots of goodies here. Steve Turner is witty, there is some sharp wordplay and he succeeds I think because he confines himself to those subjects he feels involved in. He doesn't take on the world as it were."

Roger McGough *New Musical Express*

"Within a few pages I felt that in him contemporary London may have found a lyric writer in the way that New York has so many like Steve Sondheim and Liverpool used to have Lennon."

Peter Lewis *Daily Mail*

"These poems seem to me to be the real thing, full of insights . . . His words have the ring of truth and nearness, and it is all portrayed wryly, deftly and quickly, as if light were shining round a corner."

British Weekly

"A fascinating collection of poems . . . It's artful, sharp, full of pun and fun."

Cambridge Evening News

"Steve Turner is the kind of poet that you wish they had let you study in English classes at school. His work is alive and relevant to our towerblock, commuter-orientated society. And above all, it is enjoyable. You laugh — while he tightens the thumb screw a little as he makes his point."

Buzz

"Wry, touching and sometimes uncomfortable"

Over 21